Terry Wilson lives in Adelaide, South Australia.
He has three other books published by Austin Macauley:

Fifty, Natural and *Fox Spirit.*

To Sam and Katie
partners in haiku

Terry Wilson

THE LANE AND OTHER POEMS

AUSTIN MACAULEY PUBLISHERS™

LONDON • CAMBRIDGE • NEW YORK • SHARJAH

ISBN 9781398494404 (Paperback)
ISBN 9781398494411 (ePub e-book)

www.austinmacauley.com

First Published 2023
Austin Macauley Publishers Ltd®
1 Canada Square
Canary Wharf
London
E14 5AA

Table of Contents

The Lane

1.

Stones sit on our faces by day
And are our pillows in the night
Comforts do not array themselves to us
Nor would we understand them anymore.

2.

Paper and clothing and bottles and needles
Stamped into the ground
In a million years will be the natural soil
Safe to eat with our lips.

3.

The secret book releases
A few more sentences, aphorisms
Every century
An intuitive walks into a cave
And reaches into a small cleft
May have to enlarge the cleft with a chisel or crowbar

So the hand will fit
One time they would have sliced off half the hand
Rather than hurt the stone that is holy
So the hand will fit
Perhaps what is written
Will bear no resemblance to or explicitly contradicts
What is already known
Of earlier texts gathered in the same way
From the same source
This is not information this is
A fight we must have
As it makes a little cleft in us.

4.

I was imagining the destination
As mountains or cradled by mountains
Because of the appalling obviousness of mountains in the
viewer
Worn out by years of walking
We come to a vertical wall
And that is the start
Often the end.

5.

But only a few days in
We are stopped by an outcrop of buildings
Stretching for hundreds of miles
Without any apparent way through
If we couldn't deal with *them*

What would we do with mountains
The holy way we had taken
Was sometimes a sheep track
Sometimes a four-lane highway
Invisible to environmental planners and developers
Everything is a dream
We realise after we wake up.

6.

The buildings that are seen to be blocking the view ahead
Are in fact looking with us
Are in fact showing us something
Each building has a window
And the window of one looks into the window of the next
And the last one can see everything to come
As if it was already here
Which it is.

7.

The air has cleared
And we see a clear outline
All morning it has been hidden by clouds
Clouds in us perhaps
It jumps into white view
Not just *in* the sky but *on* a layer of sky.

8.

Let's trace the red path
That leads along from the heart
Walking and walking, there it is
A narrow line that goes across our lifelines
We go on releasing the line
Length by length by hand.

I'm That Old

I lived then
I'm that baby or that kid
In those old grey pictures
Stuck by the corners in albums
Theoretically I am still alive today
Those old buildings are still standing
But renovated into colour
Everyone is on outdoor recliners
Taken outside to get the light
You couldn't shoot into the sun
We were dressed in cowboy and cowgirl uniforms
As if we'd just colonised the country
Toy guns and cats held in the same arms in the same way
Backyard fences were climbed and climbed over
And they leaned and nothing was fixed.

Leopard

1.

Please advise us
What is to be done?
Take care of business
What business do you recommend?
Business as usual

But a leopard has been let loose
And bounds almost
Into the new dispensation
Bounds us.

2.

On a hot suffer day
I typed the F key repeatedly by mistake
Though it is not adjacent on the keyboard
To the M key.

3.

Our only course of action
Is Stop
Stop and Wait
Stop and consider the flowers
Redouble our efforts, if we must have efforts
In what we hold dear here.

4.

Stand still long enough
And mountains move towards you
To see if you are ready for them
Sometimes blue mountains
Are blue butterflies
Sitting on my eyes.

Bike

I was waiting in a sunny room
The person I was waiting for was
Either late or had died
This covers all possibilities
I got a call saying I could leave
I was bicycling that day
I thought to check my tyres
Which I had forgotten to pump up
To my dismay and continued discovery of new things
I found the tyres to be completely shredded
I'd been riding on the rims
How am I not aware of these things when they happen?
The road was sunny and comfortable to ride on
I laughed at this amusing predicament
Because it was so bad
I rang for advice
But it was only of the order of, well
You'll just have to walk

We had two rooms for our first gathering
Each room was crowded
Not enough chairs so people were on the floor

It was an ideal opportunity to
Begin our proceedings with a short meditation
I explained about watching the breath
I said there are many forms of meditation
But today we would be watching the breath
I did not speak loudly
Or try to project my voice to the two rooms
Everyone will hear me
All this time my co-presenters
Were peppering me with questions
About a lost key which would have to be returned
And particulars about the food.

Guidance

For there is no time and there is no space
Everything is here in the room
The atmosphere is full of atmosphere
Pressing so on the eyes
A bell tone air
Every half hour a watch not turned off beeps
Voices with an odd Eastern European accent
Come in from Alpha Centauri and the dead
Despite the time difference
For there is no time and there is no space
Everything is here in the room
The view of rock gardens out the window
In fact the building is all windows
Extends our notion of room
Already we are questioning everything

There is an old mansion in the hills
Its name is well known to us
Once a governor's residence
Now sadly dilapidated
No flooring but a good car park
It sits on a meridian line

Making it a place of power
It is like a lightning rod for lightning running underground
It will multiply our work a thousand-fold
We will buy it
Spirit will move to make this possible
We will do it up
(with the renovation skills available in this small group
who work in offices and laboratories)
It will be an education centre for special ones
Coming into the world now
Weekend courses and retreats, possibly a school
Something big though invisible is about to happen within
twenty years
It may be very subtle but it changes everything
The world will not believe
Souls are choosing to be born 'round about now
They want to be here in body at this momentous time
Many gentle souls will be in great anguish
Adjusting again to bodies and gravity and mob violence
Such a weight of polluted energy weighs on the world
Like tar that light cannot penetrate
When I say 'Breathe' this is what we are breathing
But seriously, not in this room, we are cordoned off
And if the meridian line is actually an earthquake fault line?
It's stood there for a hundred years
It'll stand there a hundred more.

Bikes

We rode our bikes south
Till all the houses ran out
And reef and rocks started
It was uphill slog going
And free rolling feet off the pedals
Coming home
We carried spears and diving gear
Eight feet long spears that jutted out
In front of our bikes
To the consternation of anyone crossing the road
These spiked chariots bearing down
But no one crossed roads on foot then
Flies filling our faces
We got there at the white mansion
She sat alone in her acres
Surely not a house
She had a government purpose
With eyes looking out through the
Gaps between blinds
At these boys going to the beach
No sign of garden or washing on lines
A massive piece of unused land

The jewel-collecting sunbeams
At its clear centre
But no mirrored vehicles ever drove out
To drive us off
Walking now we followed the track
Outside the cyclone fence
Around the hills and slid in gravel
The steep bit
Crossed the rocks covered in shark eggs
And went into the water.

Secret Visit

One of the followers met me from my journey
At the city gates
A drawing of my face to know me by
The face that arrived was boiled red in the long crossing
And wild bearded
The picture was hardly exact either
It was a sketch made by a blind man
Then folded and folded and carried in a belt half untanned
The resemblance was if anything closer for that

He grabbed my wrist
It was the wrong wrist
I knew he was the assassin
There's an assassin in every church in formation
This was the man
What better protection in an unknown city than
A fearsome man
I was drawn by his heavy hand into the crowd

Soldiers had been alerted to my presence in the city
I heard my name spoken by every passer-by
If I responded, if I looked around

I would be dead in seconds

The man with the hand said
Out movement is in peril
You must deliver your message tonight and
Be first in line tomorrow morning when the gates open
There is no rest for the good.

Wood

Wood is slow, tree slow, and
Takes all day for one inhaling
Leaves and flowers are rather more weightless and voicey
And it is all the time with them
If you hear giggling, it'll be them
They breathe out more than they breathe in
They are air heads, the tree's air head
It takes that one long inhalation of the wood
To sink it deep in the earth
The ground filling with seeking roots
Getting into the rock seams
And after a long time the earth is made of wood

The breath in
An all-day breath
Inflates the fruit
The breath out
The fruit deflate
Sometimes some spring a leak
And whistle
As air escapes
Into air.

When You Are the River

There were no roads so
You followed the sheep
When the sheep gave out
You followed the jumper
Made from their wool
When it unpicked
To a single line of wool
Lifting in the wind which moaned
You walked along that thread off the ground
Other people who were there
Were petrified
That is they turned to stone
But you exuded confidence and
Stepped along merrily

When you are the river
Who is it
Sits on the rocks
Watching you?

The Moon in the Room

The moon set itself up
Up in a corner of the ceiling
It gazed at us with a happy benign expression
Mixing with the humans

Back to the beginning of the room
Perhaps millions of years
The moon had never spoken
What did it say now?

The sharp scratchy voice was unexpected, penetrating
From something so round
Everyone on earth heard it and
Afraid looked up
They couldn't see that reassuring old face that didn't speak
And missed it from the skies
They would have been surprised to find out
It was in our bedroom

So it said what?
Well, it made a joke about people not
Needing to turn on the light

Save power with a moon in the room
But everybody then living on earth heard it differently
With the doomsday scenario in everybody's heads
They heard that!
If the moon did say it and I missed it

It didn't mean it
Seen up close the moon has arms and hands
It made glasses shapes with its fingers
And kept us amused
In the end that was the best way to communicate
And the best thing to communicate about
Something we could understand
Of course the ceiling was wrecked
The moon rolling around with mirth and loose
Rubbing the itch on its back, the dark side.

The Elephant Poem

If you stretch an elephant
Till he is long and thin
Then roll him up
You will find it is possible
To carry him under your arm.

A Plate of Cakes

Hard to give authentic answers
From the earth
From the ground up
We are at a table outside of a café
Two strangers, we are meeting for the first and lonely time
I am an empty ear with a headful of gear
The man with me is going to break the seal on the universe
It is a square table so we are squared off
Angels gather on my shoulders like a coop of hens
And squabble and feed in my ear while he speaks
Cars rubber wheel by
I seem receptive, I'll do
Here's a surprise, a plate of cakes is brought by the waiter
I am reminded of the treats given to train dogs
The angels decide together to do a demonstration
Though I vetoed it earlier
And lift me six inches out of my metal chair
He notes this brief incident and doesn't interrupt himself
Nothing really impresses the truly spiritual
Unless it really is Truth
We all cry then or laugh.

Bin Runner

Not everything can be done by the machine
Now when the rubbish truck
Goes through, hefting the bins
In its arms
A worker in runners runs behind
Shutting all the lids
Bang bang bang
The local drinkers wide awake
Know him by now
And rubbish him good-naturedly
In the New Climate we have
New strains of deadly mosquito
Breeding in the water
That collects in bins and bin lids
There are no ponds anymore
This is what they have left
They have to be quick
They have effectively the daylight hours to
Complete the laval cycle
Then the bin is taken in
Or used as a toilet
The simple measure

Of someone to shut the lids
Before there is a cycle
Is as we would expect
Expensive and likely to be axed
In the new round.

Food

I stopped eating unnecessary meals
A cup of coffee was often enough not to feel empty
After years of food
Suddenly I was disengaged
A psychological term
I watched my dog eating
And thought we are no different
One less compulsion

I am swimming to the surface
To take a gulp of air
Or am I confused and dropping ever deeper?
Things that seem to be about life and health
Are really about death always
How not to die ever
How to take that gulp of air.

Corona

Possibly the only answer left to us
Now we are all getting ill
And stockpiling food and toilet paper
Is to sit back and look at it

If I walk, I used to think
In any direction far enough
I will go beyond the world of noise and voice
And make my enquiry there

But that takes me beyond the world altogether
Beyond enquiry and enquirer
And one night walking in that way I fell off
It is a round object after all

I knew enough to know enough
It's like trying to locate where
In the body the soul resides
Where in the world is outside?

(yes, within, I know that)

Bread

The green leaf
Surprised
Without its tree
In open air
Is suddenly
Etched in light
An infinite electricity
Joy
To power
Just the one leaf

We pick up a small
Mosaic tile
It stands in for the
Building that once stood here
We hold it up to the sun
To get that corona effect
It is like a lens
That has gone black
How can we know about the joy of a piece of ceramic
That comes back to life like this
It sees the face

That uses it to block the sun
This small shape colourfully patterned
Held between those fingers

And that dear face
The face, my face, your face
Put out your hand
She spits into the palm
She mixes it with her finger
And makes circles of it
Soon it is ready
And she closes her hand
Over mine
And bakes the mixture
What have we made?
Squished spit bread.

Frozen

Well into sleep's well and deep in sleep's deep
The cold front came in straight from the pole
I was at the screen door already
Fighting to keep it from being forced open
By what was like an ice shoulder shoving into our building
It had taken the form of the coated girth
Of a man figure
Wrenching at the door frame
Trying to gouge his fingers through the fly wire
Once in the dwelling it wouldn't be long before
The frozen attack enter our body dwelling
Right to our heart
See yourself walking on the top of a cliff
And a friend plays at pushing you
That bastard
Even if you feel suicidal
The life of the body will be shocked
And resist and refuse
Even though the intrigue of the mind
Is intrigued
In just this way our bodies fought with us
For blood and warmth

When our mind was intrigued
By what frozen would be.

Rescue

One day during the night
He got lost going to his room
And found himself in a wall cavity
Narrow and tight
It was his usual procession from the living room to bed
And how he had missed the corridor
And come in there was puzzling
Realising his error he nevertheless had to go on
It was too close to turn back
There was no one to call out to
He was alone in the house but for his deaf family
And what could *they* do,
Demolish the wall?
Hardly, he thought,
Later he was wandering about under the floor
How he got there, who can say
And later clank
He was in an air conditioner duct
At this point he panicked
He woke up and was glad to have been dreaming
But where was he?
Inside his mattress

To make this possible the springs and other fillings
Had been removed
He pushed with his arms and kicked with his legs
Trying to make a hole to leave
But now he was inside his pillow
Pillows are flat if they don't have someone,
Doesn't matter who,
Inside to bulk them up
Tonight it was him
From the inner pillow a dream goes into
The body of the one who sleeps above
He is in a state of shock by now
A lambent head rests heavily on him
He whispers, he is first considerate, then shouts
Help
Directly into the ear
This is how he came to be found
His words at first were eaten like biscuits
People are always looking for food in their sleep
They twitch and work their jaws all night as they dream
Rapid Jaw Movement RJM
But this one woke and let him out
The lambent head couldn't get back to sleep again that night
The pillow was now flat to the mattress
This is the cost of helping people who are padding out your
life.

Milk

The earth kept me on the earth
By feeding me her own milk
After two days of non-stop sucking
It was filling my throat
And I could not swallow or breathe
I was drowning on the dry ground
A god took compassion and
With a sharp stick poked holes in me
This is how I became
A spring of fountaining milk
A miracle
Wild tame animals
Come to lick with rough tongues
Pilgrims visit in buses
Some of them lick as well.

Reindeer Poem

When I stopped applying the cream to my scalp
Which had kept these things at bay so well,
The reindeer antlers soon began to reassert themselves
The rough skin I had been treating became hard and horny
And after several weeks the antlers came through
Like teeth of the young

I was going crazy rubbing my head on walls
And door frames and tree trunks
And all the paint and bark was worn off
Raising comment from my family
But their base worry was whether this would
Be part of their inheritance in the genetic scrapyard
Or contagious

I stayed out of sight
Out of human way
I couldn't go to work
Somehow I could go in through a door but not out
And got trapped in lifts and in houses
Others had to help me and they didn't like to touch the antlers
Antlers change it all

Imagine simple things like wearing a hat

I also grew reindeer wings
An innovation that has now spread to reindeer in the wild
(I don't want to say how but I'm not proud of it)
Now they migrate with the other birds
To Africa for the winter
There's a line of reindeer crap right across Europe
Marking their route and so much else.

The Ankles

I heard he was giving one of his talks and ran to the place
I was running across the centuries and across town
It was a market day as it is everyday
The streets were packed
It was a wall of walruses
And urged me on by clacking their tusks
As if I was an athlete in a race leading the pack
Because I was running some people started chasing me
So I now had a following
I broke a stone into the pan
And fried up the goodness inside

Let's find a voice that isn't my voice
It is impossible to be surprised or educated
How it is now
All taking place in my own head
Divers may not find the bottom
But the lake is not bottomless

On his hard bed
In a cement cell muttering prayers

He is lying face down so the cameras couldn't see lip
movement
It's the prayers that landed him in prison
After mortality is immortality
But he is worried about pain.

Belonging to the Moon

Belonging to the Moon
We earth-landed on an expedition
Our spacecraft died
And we couldn't get back to the Moon
Over time which is longer here
We grew hair (unusual on the Moon)
And became tangled in the earth
The Moon hearing our cries
Sent a rescue mission
Not enough fuel for the return trip
Nothing has changed
Tried drilling a long hole into a uranium deposit
And installing a tap and running a hose
The valves were leaking or something
Rescue vehicle explodes
The explosion was noticed
We are rescued by Earth instead
Live in a building
It is sited above ground open to sky fall
They won't let us inside the planet
At this stage they are keeping us on the surface
Meet fellow scientists

Discuss what to feed us

Who do we encounter going forward?
The usual answer is ourselves
Where is there room in this
For the Other?
Sometimes I am so golden
That I am amazed
And look on as a spectator
How can this unknown one
Dare show itself
In the colours that it wears?

Moon

Everyone on earth at that moment
Looked up as if someone had called their name
And waved at the moon

Though we couldn't always see it
We could point to where
It was supposed to be

Even a thought of the moon was enough
Or we drew a picture
And waved at that.

Machine

The world that doesn't breathe
Suddenly breathed slowly
For one inhalation and exhalation

He turned to me
Like a face
And showed the
Slightest
Interest in
Me

This is the world of rolling hills and rolling trees
And all that is in them

Then he looked somewhere else
And the machine started up again.

Lotus Deaths

As the virus year turns
And the plague year begins
People are learning to leave
Their bodies at will
Seeking refuge where no blight can find them
We are meditating like the ancient ones
Counting our breaths till they stop
And where the breath goes then
Well, so do we

Once you are out and
See you're you still
Why would you return?
There are a significant number
Of so-called lotus deaths
Where the body in top shape
Has just been abandoned

Most commonly
We just step out a moment
A quick peek
A quick peak

We can drop like thought through the body
As we might through anything physical
But it no longer holds us
There is no simple fall back in and
Wave the arms about I'm back
The body doesn't know us anymore
And refuses to be amazed
Left without its animation
The body begins to fail
Most of the deaths through meditation are of this sort.

Old Masters

From burning cities and burning plains
A trail leads up into the mountains
The mountains are crumbling away
Gravel, slowly
The plains will have them
But in this era the will to life still
Includes the options of mountains
And leaving is still possible
The trail is perhaps all the longer and stronger
For a good imagination
More guessed in the ground
Than can be seen
The eyes of the soul and heart
Switch over and take over
And unswervingly
Your path is that path

For one so One
Arising in one's own story
We are not surprised to see crowds of other souls
Souls and hearts
Wandering about there

Famous faces and famous beards
They know each other by the glow they show
And the words dry as dust
Dry as the place
They pray with
Ancient and continuous in history
All that under the breath chanting
Makes conversation poor
But the looks between us
Are gasping with greeting
Old friends
Touch foreheads and embrace
Like clouds falling into each other.

Old World

In the desert
The sky is a vast colon
People who stand tall enough on the ground
Their heads disappear up that rear
Finding stillness unexpectedly in all that movement
A migration of everyone is underway
They spread in grey military ranks
As soon as they get here
They get to put on the uniform
From high in the air together in lines
They look like suburbs
They go without name or face or descriptors
The God that summons them always in the present tense
Has no name or face or descriptor too
For example He is not big
Though He fills all of creation
He is intimate and close, and only that
And not only that
And not only that but the population gathered here
Swelling with new arrivals by the minute
All together like this and
Flat and stable

Make an excellent landing platform
For what comes from the sky
In the ocean it would be an aircraft carrier
Plunging and rearing
Land is better for landings.

58

Men

I started to run over
But slowed when
I saw a group of men
Around Him

Notions of a personal god
Disappeared at that moment

I watched from under a tree
Merging with its trunk,
An old friend
Once *it* was the god, the god of the grove
And intuitively I went there for refuge
Once more, still

These men I was told later
Were just as startled
When I suddenly appeared
And some of them screamed.

Spaces Left

A bird leaves a bird shape in the air when he goes
It will fill in gradually in the next hour

Animals of all stripes disappear suddenly
This is such a common experience
That our minds no longer see it
In the way that food on a plate
Is not an animal

Animals disappear right in front of us
Or they leave the room
And disappear out there
Without being seen

However it is done
Like the birds
They leave their shape behind
An air archaeologist could fill it with plaster
The moment of bodies bent over in knots

When a tree comes down
We can stand in the tree's space

Fill the space with our body
Perhaps not knowing we are doing it
And feel this resistance
Of lives passing.

Smile and Laugh

Angels when they lose their feathers
Lose their hair as well
So a knock on the casement is
Two lifelike figures
Old and bald men
Not even sure they'll be let in the door

Now they've arrived
Bowed over from the years of the weight of wings
The top of their heads precede them in the firelight
Easy enough to call this humility
But their words will be
Direct and sharp
They come as they say from a distant
City and time
Their eyes are into that distance

Even the food of that place and time isn't
Commonplace here yet
It hasn't reached us
No restaurants
No diaspora population

Just men like this

If we listen long enough
We cease to hear
And then we are told things
Welcome, sit by the fire, we say
Listen, shut up
Recognise the miracle and
Give it the intensity it requires
To surface in the world
But you are shaking with the cold, we say
We must sound like whining brats
They smile and laugh
The fire and the light go out
And the moon and stars.

Hyper

A life
Not more substantial than the movement of air
Not more substantial than a cyclone
Gathered itself unto itself
But did not do the planet thing
Stayed in the inchoate gas and dust stage
Sucking atmosphere through a straw
Time itself is subject to decay and retrograde movement
So what hope have we time babies

A bowling ball for a head
He is in no hurry about anything
At any moment other people will plug
Their fleshly fingers and opposable thumbs
Into the holes in his head
And send him rolling along a length of floor
He usually passes out before he gets to the skittles
Then he is eaten by the machine
And shat out back at the beginning
He is ninety percent solid
But is hyper about the holes
They are a metaphor for living.

Boots

In my land proof boots
I step the continents
The A-continents first
Asia Africa and others
Then I migrate to the B-continents
Then C and so on
Europe riven with rivers
And all the E-continents
Are soon upon us
All time is gathered in my hand
So wherever I visit there is plenty of time
From the ground of course they don't know what hit them
I leave a footprint the size of a state
It invariably fills with water
And there is a lake that wasn't there before
It will scratch a few geological heads
Where have we got to on our walk?
MN to W in quick order
Then we are at Z the end of the road
There is nothing beyond this
I sit on a rock there are
No buildings to sit on in these

Latter-day continents
And enjoy nothing.

Column

I lay there arms in a long position
I can make short or long as I choose

A column of air same shape as I am
Went all the way up
Very light and falling heavenwards
Through the roof and without cease

And a column of air same shape as I am
Went all the way down
Following the lines of earth force
Accumulating weight and falling heavily
Through the floor and without cease

So here we have a shaft
Not of light not of lightness
To heaven to earth
With me languishing in the middle.

Weir

I doubt that
I am hanging up here
Like a light bulb
I am falling
I am falling
Up and down and
In all directions
In total darkness
I have no context to feel this falling
No sides or edges that I can see
Going back to the light bulb
As soon as it is switched off
It falls and smashes when it hits the floor
At the same time as the light bulb
A star falls and crashes in space
Unless I crash and smash
How can I know
And if I crash and smash
Then I will know something
Today we went for a walk by the river
It was summery and shadowy
Too hot to go a long way

Bikes pinged and riders said thankyou
As we moved to single file
The river piled upwards in the middle
And only at the bank lapped at its usual place
That was because the river was full, overfull
And the weir down the river wasn't clearing
One day the infrastructure we rely on
Will stop working
Water, wood, metal, stone, or electricity
The fall that never stops
Effectively leaves us standing still
There is a dark hole in the river
That we all drain through
It is like surfing.

We Don't Know What
We Don't Know

To insert the endoscope
A medical engineer attaches a small lead weight
Called The Sinker
To bring the tube with its camera down past the gagging reflex
And into the expanse of the body
This is called Deep Diving
Then it is jiggled into final position
Called Tea Bagging
It is a precise science
The use of lead weights in medicine
Too heavy or
Too insensitive of what is jokingly called
The Manhandling of the Object
For a tight smile has not been fully eradicated in these
antiseptic white rooms
Will stretch the tube
And cause it to overshoot the mark
Once it is at the place
The sinker is let go
And it continues through its career

Finally to breach a painful exit
Similar to a kidney stone
The tube is not left in there of course
Back up the throat it leaps like a fish on a line
Snapping pictures all the way as if on holiday

Slow and halting on the stairs
You go first
Don't let me hold you up
There! I am clear behind
And free of responsibilities
How much laughter there is in running water
None of us run
Together we are a creek or a large flat river.

The Moon Reading Dante to Street People

The deep voice we can hear
Out there on the street
Is the Moon's
He has decided to enculturate
The rolling drunks
And he is starting with Dante
The whole Comedia in one night
These are the people he has got to know
They are out when he is out
And he knows the top of their heads very well
He is most affectionate at the full
Half affectionate when he is half
And feels nothing when he is little and in darkness
Right now he wants to do something about their language
Which has become quite foul
Dante will set a new standard
For language on the streets
Dante himself lost his home.

The Leaves

The leaves are panicking
Don't you hear what they are shouting!

I can't hear them
But I can see they've got the jitters

That's it, that's what I mean
Someone notices, then we all notice

The leaves are wet
Though there is no rain
Have they been crying?
Everyone cries more than we admit

How many leaves are in a forest?
Count the ones fallen on the ground as well
If they were all crying
What sort of world sees that?

Turning the question around
And what sort of world
Makes leaves cry
In the first place?

Surfacing

I am lying on a hard surface
I am lying it is a soft surface
A tabletop or floor or road
A bed or a slope of vivid grass
In either place
In neither place
Being so successfully still that
Centipedes and worms are entering me
Via my navel
It is a form of drain
They are anticipating what 'still' means
With a body laid out so
It is an act of discipline to lie here
And let that happen
Without having an opinion
Or an option
I am watching myself for aversion
And find none
Except implicitly
In watching myself for it

Is this a proper
Area of study
For a man with a job
And a family?

Relinquish

If I let it go
A core part of the path
The journey aspect for instance
And settle down in a chair
And call that spiritual
If I relinquish the journey there
On the basis that
It is already and always here now
If I relinquish one part because
It doesn't exist
Or it's a tool I
Can put down now
Does any of it stand?

Tied

My legs were tied together

My friends said
It must be restricting my freedom

I said
I can walk out of it at any time

I said
I take it off when I go to bed
And only put it on after my shower in the morning

Occasionally they pull on it like a rubber band
To make a point.

Buddha

1.

Lying on his back in bed
He reached his hand back
And touched the wall
The house was his witness

Then he climbed the ladder
And touched the ceiling.

2.

Now he is old and fat
He brings a pot
When he collects alms
He dropped his bowl and broke it
Even though it was made of iron
The world is a broken place and
A place for broken things
The pot was given to him by King Bombisara
It is made of clay and brightly painted
People who feed these recluses day after day
Know the right amount to give
They give the amount that

Would fill an alms bowl
They have not accepted
This new lesson by the Buddha
That amounts can vary.

The New Green

Walking manufactures depression
Only at the last moment of your life
You arrive at the realisation
That has been pending from the beginning
The rest of the time is time
And distance gained and persistence
So it is I see only the brown leafed
Plant when the world is contaminated by green ones
No, it's alive
Plant life has got out of the green trap
Plants everywhere will trend towards brown leaves now
Today we see the start
All this you see in passing
You go fast (to beat the weather)
So you stop
You stop to look into things
To investigate
A small molecule of you is always distressed.

Sky Shovel

On the world takes us
Demanding journeys of us
The gradient of curvation
Is along and down
We may climb the mountain or steeple
Mountains and steeples all of them go
With the run of the earth
Along and down

One day after we reach happiness
We walk along singing where all or none can hear
Or we drive at walking pace, my film crew and me
A ditch runs alongside the road
If there are dead bodies or brigands in the ditch
We never see them
Though they can soften our impact
If we slip or skid and come off the road
Happiness, rare to be so happy
Sun? Enough to catch in a bucket
And throw over the trees and see
Fruits fill out while we watch

I ask to be covered
By the colour of the sky
The colour of the sky is blue
If you put it in glass
It is the colour of glass
No colour
If you dig out with a shovel
A sky shovel
A wedge or a square of sky
And put it in the ground
To make a plant
It will make blue leaves.

Scribbled in the Air

Scribbled in the air
Needles pelts spines thorns bristles
His white mind
In a forest at night
Followed a light
It might have been the planet Venus
By a long torturous route
And he was lost
He stopped just short of a precipice
He couldn't see a way back in the dark
If he just stayed silent
He would be found
His hearing searched for someone to come
Nothing but black far as he sees
He can't see
He once reached liberation
By sneering at all that had gone before him
Now out so far
Panic grabs him
And eats him
His savage state
Is confused by a holy ringing in his head

He growls like a sad cat
Light is making the dark possible
One is the other
Here it is the absence of both
Darkness and lightness
He has somehow fallen between them

In a hand going from one finger to the next to the next
Soon we run out of fingers.

The Spike

I found a railway spike
Not far from an abandoned old line
It seemed to have something to say about religion
Something I was searching for at that time
A heavy archaeological object
I dropped it on my foot

How does religion impose its lesson?
With a love that abides no law of reason
Through boot and foot it penetrated
And nailed me where I stood
The ground was soft shale and sandy
Holding but a few stunted trees
And leaning rust fences
But I couldn't step it out
As hard as I pulled
I was secured to that place

Though I have long taken the spike out
One night it just came free by itself
As if I had matured into it
Nothing ends and I did not go though I could

A dry stream waiting on its water
Waiting for the train, I joke if asked.

The Results

If we are looking for water to sustain us
In the dry-stone places of the earth
A well is what we do
Once we puncture the stream
Surging through the rocks below
Miles below
It surges up like oil does spuming
The land is brought back to life from that underfoot rain
People move in and their cows and sheep
And eat it out and
In a generation there's no more generation
And it's back to desert again

Deep down in the spume hole
People are piling up!
Sometimes bodies come shooting up
When the water's on
People being very practical
Want to use the hole
They use it to jump in
They are struck with a bleak notion
How shallow their lives are

Next to the mysterium that
Has grown around this hole
Said to be bottomless
It is called Measuring with the Body
As they disappear down
If they are still conscious they will be acutely awake
And look up
They will see a star
The sky through the opening of the shaft so far from them
Is concentrating into a single event called a star
It hurts the eyes
To look at that bright star
And of course it injures the star
To be looked at
To be seen like that

The earth is hollow like a gourd
A few meteorites have crashed through
And rattle around inside
Now the bodies of the jumpers 'land' in here
The meteorites once brought the germs of life
Now these are the results.

Teacher

There was a moment when the whole world paused
And sighed deeply with sorrow
A Great Teacher has passed
It wasn't like the earth shook
And nobody ran out into the streets
Or had an intimation of blessing
His word was like purple fruit
Plums figs grapes
Fantastically fatally fleshy
They are lying on top of each other in the bowl
Reducing slowly over the
Hours of darkness into a syrup
Voices and engines and televisions start up again
Every noise is a person or has a person attached
Near and far they are also equidistant
They meet here
They meet in the heart.

Teachings

In the How to Be a Human Being course
We were taught to scratch ourselves
With our hands and not with our feet
The Application Form asks the following:
Name Address Age Current Species
Current Species?
How would I know?
I'll know when I pass the course
By then the answer will be human.

Centuries Old

All that has accumulated to this point
In the inner life
All sparks and shocks
Spark plugs and shock absorbers
Build like a stack of old tyres
Trying for heaven but not leaving the backyard

Who is this old man who we give welcome
And expand our shoulders to include him among us
Nay, he will be young by morning
We are all centuries old.

Mosquitos and Wasps

Mosquitos in military numbers are flying around my face
I get the high-octane cigarette lighter that I keep for this purpose out
Its flame is six inches long
I shoot it out in front of my face
Sparks show a high hit rate
Most of them run for cover by sitting on my body
Almost an impulse of compassion toward the one who kills them
Let us embrace him

On the ceiling of the cement walkway between buildings
Is a wasp nest
Residents develop a level of angst
I speak to the Pest Company about removal and relocation
Rather than eradication
Although they promote their service as contemporary and enlightened
They want to go the poison route
Contact the Local Council
If I want to save life, they advise

With the Viking raiding party
Thickset just landed on a pebbly beach with fire
Come the Viking farmers
Who settle and intermarry with the existing population
In two ways the Viking genes burn through the gene pool.

The Hands

A horseshoe of people
Grows out of the darkness of the earth
Travellers on horseback
Too dark to see from their faces
If they are bandits or holy pilgrims
They do not live somewhere
No matter how still they appear
They have a course and continue on

We can focus just on their hands
Gripping
Loosening their grip
Losing their grip
Getting a grip
As they ride
On journeys that are every day and months and years long

Suddenly there is a fright we can't see or hear
Hands jump up in horror
Next moment

All hands become birds
Snapped up in a startled mob
Wheeling around above.

Want

'Want' is a word that crops up often in human deliberations
We wanted to mine lava direct from the volcano

We lowered our buckets on their long lines
Deep into the kicking red liquid rock and other minerals

The buckets weren't made to volcano specifications
And vaporised almost immediately

Fire ran up the long lines
We released them just in time

So we lowered some of the men by the ankles
But they weren't as long as the long lines

But if we left them there
They stretched.

Defence

When I was a child in bed at night
It happened sometimes
In the room
In the darkness
There was breathing
An ankle cracked then nothing
I froze pretending to be asleep rigid
My bow and arrow in bed next to me
One day locked in my room for a nap
I threw my bow out of the window
With the words 'Rescue me'
Written on it in big childish letters
Of course only the family passed by there
But at night it meant I had given away
My only hope
My only defence.

Nest of Boxes

Inside all the boxes
Was another box
It never ended
There was a heart in there too
A beating heart
And inside the heart was another heart
It never ended either

Along a Length of Cord I Inched

Along a length of cord I inched
Wherever I stopped
We call that day
This is the life
A bright light shone
Like a torch
Often directly in my eyes
Teaching them to see
Everywhere else on the cord
Which resembled the pull of a blind
Let's not sugar it
Was dark forest
And appalling fear

Horse

I place my hand on his face to reassure him somewhat
I slip the reins and off he goes
White into darkness
Now he is an ordinary horse, ordinary in human terms
When I found him, he was standing stranded in mid-air
Tethered to a tree, a forlorn looking tree
Also suspended in mid-air
Both in their ways distressed, afraid of heights, even the minor
heights we are talking of here
Nothing to give them footing
I walked up and untied him, them
That I could walk up didn't surprise me till later
The tree immediately slipped sideways and
Crashed to earth only a few feet down
Its burden done
And etherealised to atoms, to nothing
The horse as I said running free
In the air the range of restriction is extensive
On the ground, green and mounded world
There are laws, laws because freedom and wildness are
implied
A horse can run.

Word Song

First there was to be no speaking
Keep quiet everyone

The Lord spoke to us
In an inner loud voice
We coloured with embarrassment
We had to hush him
Though what he said was lovely

Now the world turns
Or we turn in the world
We are using words again
They've become the means to the end
The how of what
The what of what

Line

He let out a long fishing line
And walked along it
Making it his life's path

Most of the time it
Followed the roads
And he had to dodge traffic

He didn't consider himself
To be a fish
It is simply that fishing line
Is a fine material
Strong and long lasting

This is how he would
Like his doctor to remember his life
Not as a fish

Gourd

It's autumn every day of the year in the valley of death
Why be shy about such terms and place names
Leaves already broken off
Already on the ground
Talk among themselves, never with us
Of the unparalleled freedom they now have
But all the same edge like slippery dogs
Away from your walking
Because you seem to enjoy their crackle
Beautiful, sunny
A shower of leaves
Touching you lovely
Death is always sewn into the equation
What is biological soon becomes geological
I can't put a name to a flower
Except roses, daffodils, soursobs, the ones I
Learned to say when I was a child
A red custardy flower
Looks like it is looking at me
A sentinel flower.

The Once

The road of sticks
Threads its way
Through the unbending trees
In darkness and shadow and sad story
For many miles
Then peters out
It begins to rain
The sticks wash away in the deluge
Under the road of sticks
We see a road of paper
A refinement of the first
Of course it tears
It is used only the once
Keep going forward
If you want to see your way
You are the once.

The Personality Test

Perhaps the days were different lengths then
One day only a few hours
The next day extending over several years
Overall I lived longer than a regular clock-based lifespan

It was a time of feeling
And feeling my way
I believed in contradictory and different things
As they delighted me and each other

In the world of nature and second nature
I saw a star moving in me
Part of anatomy and part of breathing
It sat on my brow and on my crown
When I gazed up at the sky
It rolled across my face
And teetered on my chin

Now the world is measurable
Square and round
The town is square
The world is round

We'll never get out
We'll never get off.

When You Are the River

There were no roads so
You followed the sheep
When the sheep gave out
You followed the jumper
Made from their wool
When it unpicked
To a single line of wool
Lifting in the wind which moaned
You walked along that thread off the ground
Other people who were there
Were petrified
That is they turned to stone
But you exuded confidence and
Stepped along merrily

When you are the river
Who is it
Sits on the rocks
Watching you?

Baby Snake

At our first house in town
Out of the dark gap between houses, next door and us
A gap only enough to fit a hand
How far do I think I can reach in there
I saw a thick worm
Length about two inches
Emerge for the sun light and warmth
The house had been empty for weeks so it
Was the first day of not being safe
Perhaps living in the dark it had evolved blindness
Its skin-coloured eyes coupling and uncoupling
Like baby hands
I thought it was a young snake
It was too small to see feet
It may have been a lizard holding its feet tight to itself
Like a fish caught gasps
Frightened

We called out the snake catcher
Two inches is an easy job for one of that trade
With his sacks and reinforced gloves
He couldn't locate our snake in the rough earth off the path

But told enough about small
Being especially venomous for snakes
To leave me looking incessantly
In that little stretch of rubble along the foundations
I parked my bike there
Never a puncture that might have been fangs
We were in that house for a year
It was pretty quiet in terms of danger.

Bandaged

My hand was bandaged when I arrived
At the accident site
Because of a recurrent injury

You won't be much help
Said my patient

Are you kidding, You have bandages
All over your torso, legs and both your hands are strapped up
I'm minimal compared to you
I can change your dressings no problem
Plus it's me, here I am, no one else
Came when you called
There is a world of people
But I'm the one who responded
That's everything

Now just put your finger
On this knot please
While I tighten it
Don't let it slip.

Botanic Gardens

On a hot summer day
We are the dead ones
Drifting in the black shadows
We have arrived at our destination
We have done what we set out to do
There is nowhere further to go
Perhaps we set the gate too soon
We may live like this for another thirty years
Sheltering under lofty trees
Our own gentleness, which is genetics
Brings us up short
There is no end of land or
Natural barrier in the land
Just a sign
Go No Further
Not in this life
It flickers up in the blood
What is left of blood
There is no going back either
No erasing and rewriting
Once at the high water mark you stay there
Who says time doesn't stand still

First Mountains

When you start there are mountains to cross
They dominate the earth before you
The climb up there among the clouds
One can lose sight of the journey
Counting the number of rungs on a ladder
Beyond one
You arrive in the pure land
The sky is pink all day
And there are peaches instead of apricots
In other respects it is the same as what you left
You seem incapable of surprise.

I Hid My Head

I hid my head in peasant clothing
And took to the road on foot
Foreign troops roving in the countryside
Looking for adventures
Often pulled me over to have a little fun
Poked me with their rifles and sticks
And would have finished me off
But I was too effacing to take seriously
I smiled and nodded in agreement
And picked up what they threw down
Even bowed slightly when they let me go
But they must have known from
The shape of my face and brow
Like a smooth stone
I was capable of abstract thought
And able to dominate them with my character
I stood to one side as they passed
Because it made good military sense to do so.

Like a Searchlight I Am Stillness

Somebody killed me
But nothing was lost
I still carried the same body around
But pushed in a shopping trolley rather than wear it
The same things worried me
And kept me awake at night
Schedules and timelines and output
The only difference was
It always was night
I have the shades of water on my face
I splash but I can't splash anything
Nothing responds or gets wet
Kicking and splashing as if it was a river
Shudder, writhe and wring
My hand breaks into nothing
And breaks out of nothing
And questions its own existence

Like Ink

like ink I was being sucked into a hole
parts of my body were stretching and going in
I was terrified all teeth
everything I had read to give me foundation
and a petty contempt for fear
it was those loose pages
that
flapped
like birds
out of the black well

Lion and the Anchorite

The lion brings something dead to the door
The Rule of our Order
Forbids to stimulate the flesh with flesh
I am the local lord of the Lord
My responsibility though I be eaten lies in this
I head butt the poor creature
Then punch him with a right hook
He totters looks amazed ashamed
A little roar comes out that is pathetic
I smile and break my face
I am weak at the moment I need to be strong
He was already fully grown
When I found him lying in his tears in a depression of the land
Here was the wild heart I was given to conquer
First it was my heart now mercy had given me his
The porridge I fed him
Clearly hadn't deflected his cruel nature
As today's events have shown
Hadn't defeated nature
Weaned him
I place him in exile
Away he breaks into a run

Tomorrow I'll wake while it is still dark and icy
And find him curled up below snoring and having a dream
Warming the cell
For now he goes away with a sore head a sore face
Looking very sorry
I looked and looked at that
Torn rag of red dead ooze
He left on my step
He returned I let him swallow it.

Look, I'm Alive

Doors smash shut
Metal doors crash shut
People stuck outside use clubs
Fashioned from a broken chair
Or else their heads
They ought to have their heads red
And shout moral mortal threats
To be let in
Last time they were let in
They were banned and let out
They were lambs
But they grinned too widely
Showing their bright lips
And made some bad wolfsome jokes
Now they club the door
And shout victimised
Till the police come
To zither their songs of the gutter.

Lots of Holes

It is refreshing going outside when
It is still early and the air is cool

It hasn't made up its mind yet
To become day

Sometimes the moon is out too
And is squashed like a peach

In houses of the far past
There was not a clear difference
Between inside and outside

Houses had lots of holes in the walls
As many as ten thousand
Letting in the cool air

Houses were made of wickerwork then
Or holes were left from arrows
After the sheep raids

Lines of light, ten thousand of them perhaps
Created beautiful patterns
With the dust in the air
Though the general impression
Was one of darkness and by our standards
Desolation

Smoke from cooking fires
Could easily find its way out
But tended to hang around in the house
Babies cried then as now

If it got too bad
The family could roll the wicker hut
Onto its back and let it air
Let the sun attack all its dark secrets

From the beginning of civilisation to the end of civilisation
Going outside and breathing
Has saved us.

Mountain

If we go there
A mountain appears before us out of sheer wonder
Mists soften any edges
As we climb we enjoy the view
It doesn't allow you to see straight down
Clouds soft and bubbly
Strategically stand between us and a long tumble
Screeching baboons would normally
Bale us up for sandwiches
Here under the Buddha's ferns they become
Kindly sagely customer service baboons
Take us by the hand on the difficult stretches
Their hair beading in the wet like ours
Soon we are at a pavilion with cushions and a snooker table
As well as tea there is an assortment of wines.

Nest

Around the house is an outer wall
Then a courtyard wall
Then a green wall of vines
Boxes within boxes
We have soundproofing, weatherproofing, whether proofing
We the family sit
Right in the middle
Equidistant from it all.

October of That Year

In October of that year
It rained and it was cold
Usually the sun comes out of winter
And from one day to the next
We have summer
The month's average rainfall fell in the first week
And the reservoirs and farmers were full
It was very wet rain
And it reached all the way to the ground
It also rained inside the houses
And inside the buildings of the weather bureau
People wore rubber raincoats

And rather enjoyed bumping into each other
And bouncing off
Complete strangers would take
Run ups at each other
And laughed till tears
Rained out of their eyes

In the slippery conditions
They ran around like headless hens
And rolled around like henless heads
Most people didn't have a hen
And had to make do with their heads.

Once the Sun

Once the sun is a glob of white
Like something a bird did
It diameters your eye
And pulls you in like a fish
Except you are perfectly calm
Up so high in the air
Not thrashing about
In buckets and baskets
Enjoying everything
Everything that ends

A loud whistle on my doorstep
Is a test whistle it
Is not intended for people who have houses
To cower in it
Is for the streets
Perhaps testing the acoustics of spaces
Where people talk at a distance from each other
A laugh becomes a cough then a cough up
The street outside our house
Is covered with the insides of people

Predilection

I developed a predilection for mountains
How they look in pictures and what height means
But I never climbed one

Once we step onto the path
It's mountains all the way
And llamas and lamas

Life might start at the harbour
But it tends to the interior
So that boat, put it down

Even on flat ground
Fields and soft weather
We can fall off

Even on the plain
We can fall a vertical death
And never be found

We catch buses and sit in cars
We ride on donkeys and take photos
Take a bullet train to get there

Our friends who stay with us
All the way up to the beginning
Wave us off, wave us on

Watch every day through
A telescope or telephoto lens
From the drinks tent

There's a part where we are still just visible
Dots leaving tracks behind us
A cloud tucks us in.

Sky

A strong wind blows this fellow off the earth
This rope is attached to a pole at one end
And to his ankle at the other

The earth is always the hero in encounters of this type
The sky, up in the sky, the tree line, the coins falling out of
his pocket
None of these figures as much as the ground
No one gets away, right?
But for a few minutes until the wind lets go
Just one
It's him.

We Will Always Find People

The ocean underneath our feet
Is salt water as we would expect
But only for the first five or six miles depth
There is after that a layer
Of the purist drinking water
As though the ocean sits or swims in a lake
A dark and silent never visited place
And a further few miles again
Who knows, we might strike air
A pocket of air surviving at the bottom of the sea
And where there is air
A sky surging and always black this far down
We will always find people
Who have wandered here
And make their home
So there are very likely towns and villages and fields
A fresh water species of lantern fish
Make the planets and stars
But the people themselves have
Grown phosphorescent too
More like the sun

Surprise

White lights and white circles,
Don't rush to the verb
That finishes this experience

For as long as they stay
Let us try to stay too

In the midst of this wonder
An anxious thought called next
Draws one eye then the other eye

When we look back
The lights and circles are still round
But we know what they are now
And we are surprised that we were ever surprised.

Take Flower

I take flower from the Garden of Eden
And press it in the pages of a book
To flower is a source
And much more than the book, any book
And in time the Garden of Eden flower
Takes the leaf of the pages
And overprints them
With flower
The book is now useless as a book
But something to hold in the hand
Unique and a prize
It is all the more remarkable
That in the same world this exists
Voices from the seventh circle of hell
Rise out of the black hole in the street
Such sad flowers they are
Caught in violence
On the ground to the kicks of others
In a wild hypnotic frenzy
Acting bad in a mob is transcendent and forgetful
They are pages of the same book
There is only one book

Less quiet, less secret, but more than loud voices
We might be the same thing as the other
Blessings to everyone.

Legs and Arms

The sun comes up about midnight
As is the custom here
And goes down again by morning
We go off to work in milky darkness
And most often sleep through the fire flare at night
Which is just our normal
The star constellations we all know from books
Are away on the edge of our sky
Pleasing the world above
The northern hemisphere I mean
Our sun is a different shape too
It is as though a hand squeezed it
It is like a column of unbearable light
Straight up and down
Like god looking directly at us
Straight up and down
Or sometimes it is just the opposite
A horizontal light
Extending along the edge of the world we see
The horizon
And not coming any further
Stars and the sun which is a star too

Are emotionally distant where we live
As well as being miles distant
Our hearts are squeezed
Into that column shape
Or they are asleep
Arms and legs sprawled over the horizon
We don't have bleeding hearts
So they can do what they want
Suddenly on a rare day
A ray from the sun
Will shoot across the many miles to here
Between two mountains it may be
Squished into coherence momentarily
'All that is hot' scorches the land
It looks like road a straight roman road revealed
That goes to us from the sun
One doesn't want to get zapped by that beam
But afterwards we have something that has opened in us
But it's still a long way
If we go

Valleys

Suddenly we were in the All
Suddenly ends forever
We yell like mountaineers
Cannot make ourselves heard over the sirens
Hospitals have arrived to take us to the ambulances
There are no mountains
People want to see mountains but live in valleys
Valleys are therefore what we see
There is a fine view of valleys from ground level
The air is thin and needs thinking about as we take steps
Like we are up high
But it is the yelling the yodelling the packing with laughter
Making us light-headed and short of breath
We yell like mountaineers
(across the abyss)
Cannot make ourselves heard above the sirens
Yet if we mutter and curse even benignly
Under our breath
They hear that the next town over
Nestling in the valley
The tight wind suffused with everything
Suffuses with everything

Collects us
Tree me why don't you
Yellow and gold and dun
Leaves falling
Yelling abuse in our knockabout happy way
So objectional it's wonderful!

Walking Towards a Mountain

All I am interested in
Is walking toward a mountain

If it is hidden from view
Behind another closer mountain
Or in cloud
I draw an arrow in the gravel
When I stop for the night
In case I turn around in my sleep

Best of all is seeing it get larger every day
Those days add up into the weeks and months
Then the big immanent
The mountain swims up to me
Having been so reticent

Since that time
It has dropped below the horizon
So I draw an arrow in the gravel
Gods are twisting the paths like wool
Writhing them off the ground
We are walking across gods and over gods

They are their own geography
Some like it some do not
One minute bliss the next avalanche
I have a map I was given in terror by a stranger in a bazaar
Who was running from someone when he found me
It is drawn in milk
The details of roads and landmarks
Have turned sour have turned into yoghurt
Milk was all the monk had to write with
Its smell has transferred itself to my whole being and
Rings in my sleep
So I do not sleep well
The map with all its hallucinatory material ohh!
Makes sense and is increasingly accurate
Impossible and impassable are the same word
Once we wake up we're dreaming.